C

Places the Stars

A Native American Legend

by Meish Goldish

illustrated by Darrin Johnston

Harcourt
SCHOOL PUBLISHERS

Printed in the United States of America

ISBN 10: 0-15-351129-X
ISBN 13: 978-0-15-351129-5

Ordering Options
ISBN 10: 0-15-350603-2 (Grade 6 On-Level Collection)
ISBN 13: 978-0-15-350603-1 (Grade 6 On-Level Collection)
ISBN 10: 0-15-357990-0 (package of 5)
ISBN 13: 978-0-15-357990-5 (package of 5)

2 3 4 5 6 7 8 9 10 179 12 11 10 09 08 07

Characters

Narrator	Wolf 1	Bear 1
Coyote	Wolf 2	Bear 2
Meadowlark	Wolf 3	
	Wolf 4	
	Wolf 5	

Narrator: Long ago, there were five wolves who were brothers. They always traveled and hunted together. When they had meat, they shared it with their cousin, Coyote. One night, Coyote saw the wolves perched on a mountaintop. All five were looking up at the sky. Coyote climbed the mountain and joined the wolves.

Coyote: What are you looking at, my cousins?

Wolf 1: Oh, nothing, Coyote.

Narrator: The following night, Coyote saw the wolves back on the mountaintop. They were looking up at the sky again. Coyote was very curious.

Coyote: What are all of you staring at up there?

Wolf 2: It's really nothing, Coyote. It's nothing at all.

Narrator: Night after night, the same thing happened. Coyote saw the wolves looking up at the sky, and though he always asked gingerly, they refused to say what they were staring at.

Coyote: Please, dear cousins, please tell me. What is it in the sky on which you thrive? What is it that interests you so much? I will be greatly indebted to you if you tell me.

Wolf 3: Honestly, we are not looking at anything.

Coyote: Cousins, I do not like that you are keeping a secret from me! I find it unbearable not knowing what it is. Please tell me what it is you see up there!

Wolf 4: Brothers, we may as well tell Coyote. I don't think it will do any harm.

Coyote: You're right, you're right. It will not do any harm.

Narrator: Coyote couldn't wait to learn what the wolves were looking at.

Wolf 5: Fine, Coyote, I will tell you. Every night, we see two animals high in the sky. They are very far away out of our reach. That is a problem for us. It makes us feel dissatisfied as hunters.

Coyote: My cousins, that is no problem at all. I have the ideal answer. I am optimistic that I can get you up into the sky to see the animals. That way you will be close enough to hunt them.

Wolf 1: You can? How would you be able to do that?

Coyote: It's simple. Just wait here for a minute or two.

Narrator: Coyote ran down to his cave. He found his bow and an abundant number of arrows. He carried them back to the mountaintop.

Wolf 2: What do you plan to do with your bow and arrows, Coyote?

Coyote: Watch this, my cousins.

Narrator: Coyote shot an arrow upward. It flew high and stuck into the sky. He shot a second arrow. It flew high and stuck into the first arrow. Then he shot a third arrow that stuck into the second. He shot arrow after arrow after arrow. Each one stuck into the one before it. In time, a long ladder of arrows reached from high in the sky all the way down to the mountaintop.

Coyote: There, I am done. Now we can all climb to the sky to see the animals.

Wolf 3: Is it safe to climb your ladder, Coyote?

Coyote: Oh, yes, my prudent cousins, it is quite safe. However, it is a long trip.

Narrator: Coyote and the five wolves began the long, arduous journey toward the sky. They climbed the ladder all day and into the night. They climbed the next day and night as well. After several more days and nights, they finally reached the sky. The wolves looked at the two animals they had seen from the mountaintop.

Wolf 4: Look, brothers! The animals we saw from earth are bears. They are two large bears!

Coyote: Do not go near them. They look dangerous!

Narrator: The two younger wolves were quite cocky. They were not afraid of approaching the two bears. They began to move toward them.

Wolf 1: Stop, young brothers! You heard Coyote's demands. Do not go near the bears! Stay far away!

Narrator: The two young wolves did not stop. They sat near the bears and stared at them. The two bears remained stationary and stared right back at the two young wolves.

Wolf 4: Look, older brothers, it is apparent that the bears are harmless. Do not be afraid.

Wolf 5: Yes, brothers, please come over and sit with us.

Narrator: The three older wolves saw that the bears were safe, indeed. They moved closer and sat quietly near the large bears. Only Coyote didn't come over. He stayed far away.

Wolf 2: Aren't you going to join us, Coyote?

Wolf 3: Yes, Coyote, do come over and sit here with us.

Coyote: No, thank you, my cousins. Those bears appear friendly, yet I still do not trust them. However, I must admit that you and the bears look comfortable together. It's truly a nice picture of communal peace and happiness.

Narrator: Just then, Coyote had an idea. He began to think to himself.

Coyote: They all look so nice sitting there like that. I feel such bliss just gazing at them. I think I will leave the wolves and bears this way for everyone on earth to enjoy. When people see them, they will say, "There's a story about that picture." The people on earth will then tell a story about me.

Narrator: As a result, Coyote left the five wolves sitting peacefully with the two bears. He began to climb down his ladder. He took out each arrow along the way.

Wolf 1: Cousin Coyote, where are you going? Are you leaving us stranded here?

Coyote: Yes. Do you wish to return to earth with me?

Wolf 2: No, Coyote, we are all happy here.

Narrator: As Coyote climbed down from the sky to the mountaintop, the image of the bears and the wolves receded. From earth, he admired the picture he had left above. Today the picture still looks the same. People on earth call it the Big Dipper. It has seven stars. Together, they form the shape of a cup with a long handle. Such a cup is called a "dipper."

Wolf 1: I am part of the handle.

Wolf 2: I am, as well.

Wolf 3: I am, too.

Wolf 4: I am on one side of the cup.

Wolf 5: As am I.

Bear 1: I am on the other side of the cup.

Bear 2: I am also on the other side of the cup. We bears point toward the North Star.

Narrator: Coyote stared for a long time at his picture in the sky. He liked it so much that he added more stars around it. Then he made a big road called the Milky Way across the sky with the stars he had left over.

Coyote: Now I am done. The stars in the sky make a beautiful picture. Everyone on earth will surely admire it for a long time. I want them to know that I was the one who made this great picture.

Narrator: Coyote knew exactly how to do that. He paid a visit to his bird friend Meadowlark.

Meadowlark: Hello, Coyote! How good to see you again! What brings you to my neck of the woods?

Coyote: Meadowlark, look up at the sky. Do you see that beautiful picture made of stars? Since you stay awake all night, will you please spread the word? Tell everyone that I am the one who created that picture. That way, my name will forever be entwined with the Big Dipper.

Meadowlark: It will be my pleasure to do so, Coyote.

Narrator: To this very day, Meadowlark sings the praises of his friend Coyote each and every night. He tells everyone that Coyote shaped the Big Dipper in the northern sky.

Think Critically

1. Why are the wolves unhappy that the animals in the sky are so far away?

2. What are the wolves looking up at in the night sky in the beginning of the story?

3. If you were one of the wolves, would you have stayed in the sky or returned to earth with Coyote? Explain your answer.

4. Why does Coyote call on Meadowlark to spread his message?

5. What message about peace does this legend suggest?

Science

Star Report Use an encyclopedia or other book to learn more about the Big Dipper or another constellation. Write a brief report on your findings. Include a drawing that shows the positions of the seven stars.

School-Home Connection Tell your family the Native American legend of Coyote placing the stars. Talk about the things each of you would like to be remembered for in the future.

Word Count: 1,309